You're Some CROOKED!

Quirky words from Newfoundland and Labrador

Written and Illustrated by:
Necie

DRC Publishing
3 Parliament Street
St. John's, NL A1A 2Y6
Telephone (709) 726-0960
Email: info@drcpublishingnl.com
Website: www.drcpublishingnl.com

Library and Archives Canada Cataloguing in Publication

Necie, author, illustrator
    You're some crooked / Necie.

ISBN 978-1-926689-88-3 (pbk.)

    1. English language--Dialects--Newfoundland and Labrador--
Juvenile literature. 2. Newfoundland and Labrador--Social life and
customs--Juvenile literature. I. Title.

PE3245.N4N43 2015   j427'.9718   C2015-902255-X

Published 2015

Printed in Canada

We acknowledge the financial support of the Government of Canada through the Canada Book
Fund for our publishing activities.

You're Some CROOKED!

Quirky words from Newfoundland and Labrador

Written and Illustrated by: Necie

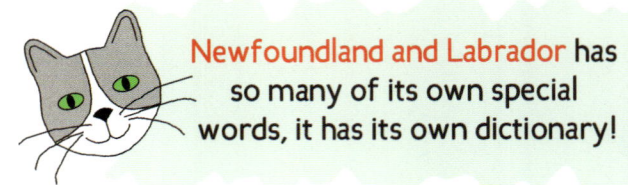

Newfoundland and Labrador has so many of its own special words, it has its own dictionary!

In Newfoundland and Labrador
A place along the ocean shore

Some words you might not understand
In this unique and special land

Perhaps you'd like to learn a few
Like Doughboy, Chummy and Whole Slew!

Read on!

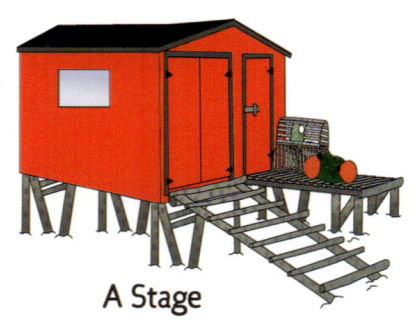

A Stage

If you are crooked, you might be TANGLY too, which means you will argue or fight over just about anything!

If you're grumpy, sour and snappy
And you're cranky and unhappy

Your lovely smile is upside down
It's turned into an angry frown

If you are in a nasty mood
And only feel like being rude

You're CROOKED

A Killick

3

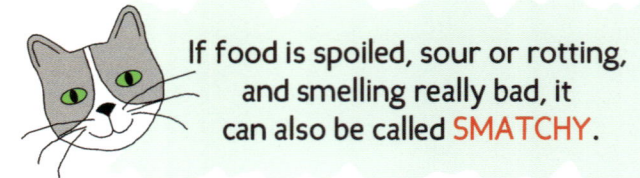
If food is spoiled, sour or rotting, and smelling really bad, it can also be called SMATCHY.

If food's no longer good to eat
Reminding you of smelly feet

The sour smell is kind of sickly
And your stomach's turning quickly

When stinky food is sort of rotten
And your appetite's forgotten

It's FOUSTY

Figgy Duff

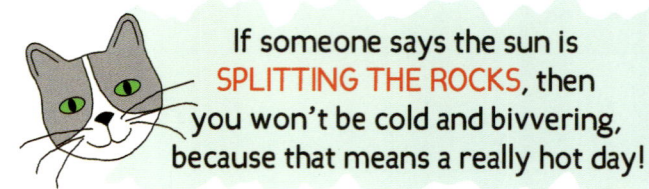

If someone says the sun is SPLITTING THE ROCKS, then you won't be cold and bivvering, because that means a really hot day!

If your body starts to shiver
And your bottom lip to quiver

When wooly socks upon your feet
Don't seem to keep in any heat

If all your teeth begin to click
You really need to warm up quick

You're BIVVERING

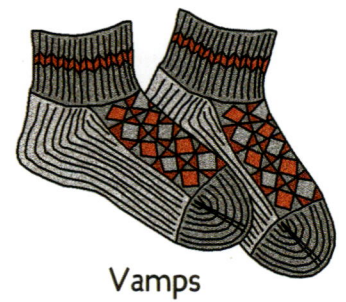

Vamps

7

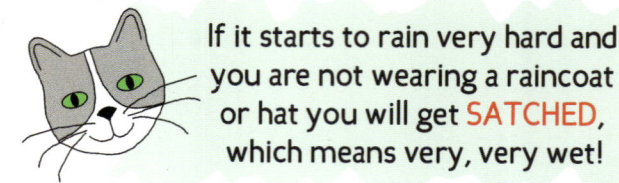

If it starts to rain very hard and you are not wearing a raincoat or hat you will get SATCHED, which means very, very wet!

If the weather's kind of foggy
And the ground is extra soggy

And all the air is sort of gray
You really can't see far away

It feels like rain is going to pour
But it's just mist and nothing more

It's MAUZY

A Sou'wester

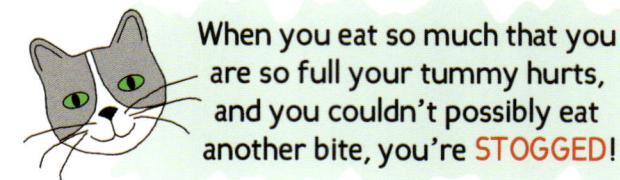

If you've had a meal so yummy
You completely filled your tummy

Perhaps pea soup and doughboys too
Or fish and brewis or pot of stew

And you completely cleaned your plate
You can't believe how much you ate

You've had a SCOFF

Fish and Brewis

11

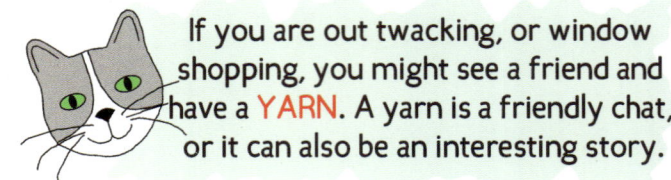

If you are out twacking, or window shopping, you might see a friend and have a YARN. A yarn is a friendly chat, or it can also be an interesting story.

If you decide to go to town
To visit stores and look around

You may not buy a thing today
You just admire each display

At each and every store you stop
But not to buy, just window shop

You're TWACKING

Mummers

13

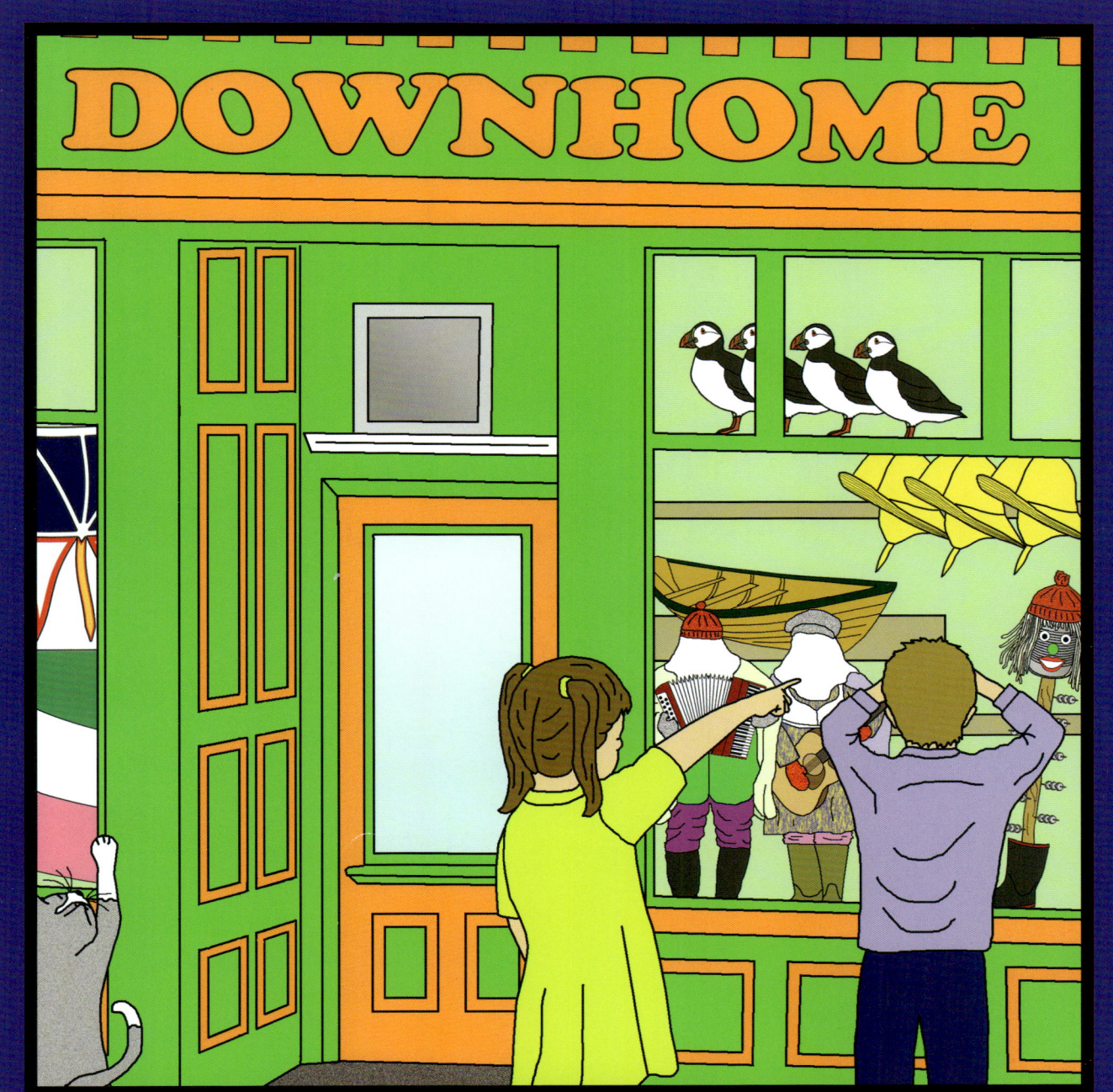

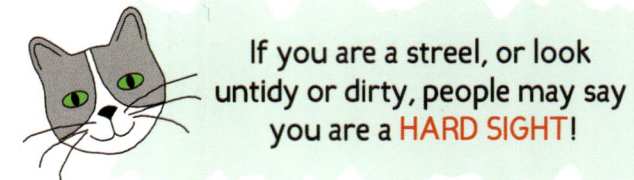

If you just really didn't care
To wash your face or comb your hair

If your clothes are always rumpled
And your shoes are worn and crumpled

You always look like such a mess
And really don't mind how you dress

You're a STREEL

Slip Shods

You might go out BUM-BYE,
which means later.

If you decide to go somewhere
You're not quite sure when you'll get there

It seems you really can't decide
Just how long you'll stay inside

You might go later in the day
Exactly when you just can't say

You'll go THE ONCE

A Mug Up

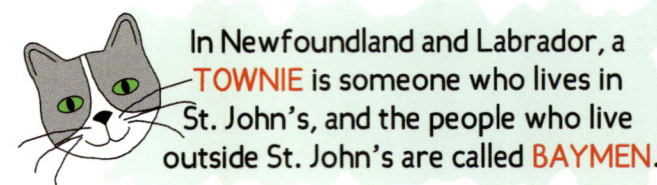

In Newfoundland and Labrador, a TOWNIE is someone who lives in St. John's, and the people who live outside St. John's are called BAYMEN.

If there's a stranger at your door
You've never seen his face before

He's not a Townie, there's no doubt
And not a Bayman you find out

If he has not lived here before
In Newfoundland and Labrador

He's a CFA or COME FROM AWAY

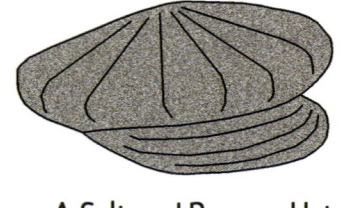

A Salt and Pepper Hat

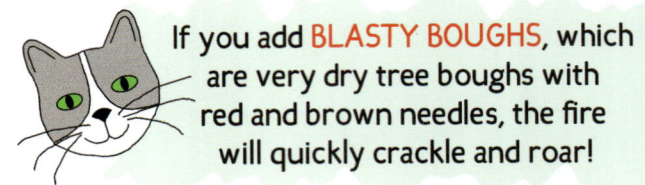

If you add BLASTY BOUGHS, which are very dry tree boughs with red and brown needles, the fire will quickly crackle and roar!

If you're outside and spot a fire
And there are pots hung from a wire

The flames are burning warm and high
And flankers drift up to the sky

You see a very friendly bunch
They're boiling tea and making lunch

It's a BOIL UP

Flankers

21

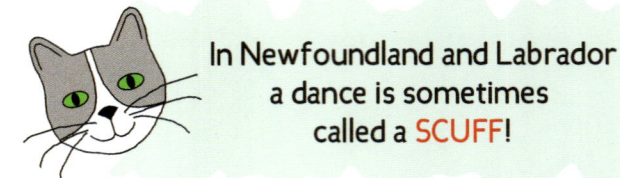

In Newfoundland and Labrador
a dance is sometimes
called a SCUFF!

When all the daily work is done
And neighbours gather for some fun

In someone's kitchen or a hall
In winter, summer, spring or fall

They have a scoff and have a scuff
Tell jokes and sing and other stuff

It's A TIME

An Ugly Stick

23

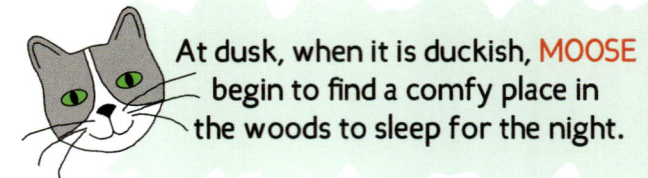

At dusk, when it is duckish, MOOSE begin to find a comfy place in the woods to sleep for the night.

If you are out that time of day
When evening's soon to go away

The sun is crawling into bed
The moon is not yet overhead

It's not quite day and not quite night
It's not quite dark and not quite light

It's DUCKISH

A Moose

25

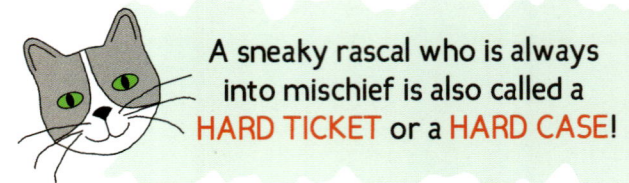

A sneaky rascal who is always into mischief is also called a HARD TICKET or a HARD CASE!

If you've been known to trick a friend
You think that rules are meant to bend

If you are a mischievous one
A rascal who tells lies for fun

If you cause trouble every day
You'd rather scheme and tease than play

You're a SLEEVEEN

Toutons

27

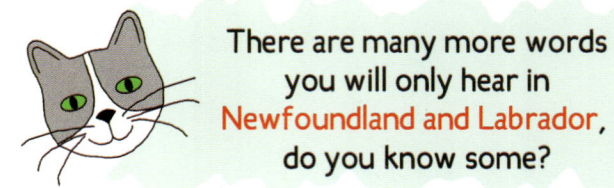
There are many more words
you will only hear in
Newfoundland and Labrador,
do you know some?

If you knew words inside this book
You did not need a second look

You've been out on a mauzy day
And had a boil up by the bay

You've had a scoff, you've had a scuff
You bivver when the weather's rough

Then you are here
or were before
In *Newfoundland and Labrador*!

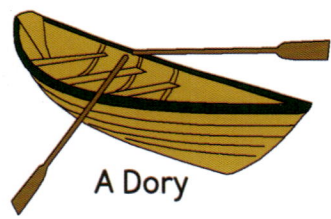
A Dory

Picture Glossary

Stages are very important buildings to fishermen. They are built next to the ocean. Here fishermen keep their boats and fishing tools.

A **Killick** is a handmade anchor made from a large stone and sticks.

A traditional Newfoundland pudding made with raisins, put in a bag and boiled in a pot is called **Figgy Duff**.

Vamps are short hand knit cozy warm wool socks.

A waterproof hat with a wide brim worn by fishermen is called a **Sou'wester**.

Picture Glossary

Fish and Brewis is a traditional meal of boiled salt fish, crispy fried pieces of pork called **scrunchions**, and soaked hard bread.

People who dress up in disguise to visit neighbours' homes during Christmas are called **Mummers**. They entertain folks!

Shoes made by cutting the legs off old rubber boots at the ankle and just leaving the part for the foot are called **Slip Shods**.

A **Mug Up** is a lunch or snack that is often enjoyed with a nice hot cup of tea.

A **Salt and Pepper Hat** is hand knit and gets its name because the wool used to make it looks like salt and pepper mixed together!

Picture Glossary

Flankers are sparks from a fire that burn out as they drift up into the sky. They look very pretty at night!

A decorated musical instrument made of a long stick and anything that will make noise, like bottle caps, is called an **Ugly Stick**.

Moose are very large animals. They are excellent swimmers and they can run quite fast too!

Toutons are pieces of bread dough fried golden brown and served with molasses – which is also known as **lassie**. Yum!

A **Dory** is a small wooden fishing boat. Fishermen used oars to row the dory.

Odds and Ends

Bakeapple – Berries that grow in marshy places in Newfoundland and Labrador. They are quite yummy and can be very hard to find!

Brewer – A very nice, calm weather day that occurs just before a big storm.

Chummy – Can be anything! If someone forgets the name of something, they will call it a "chummy". Sort of like a "thing-a-ma-jig" or a "whatchmacallit"!

Doughboy – Fluffy bread dumplings that are cooked in soup and stew.

Flake - A platform built on poles to spread salted fish on to dry in the warm sun and fresh air.

Gut-foundered – Really, really, really hungry!

Livyer – Someone who has lived in Newfoundland and Labrador all their lives.

Nipper – A mosquito.

Racket – An argument or a fight. It can also mean quite a lot of noise.

Whole Slew – A lot of something

You're Some Crooked – If you are crooked, you are in a bad mood. If someone says "you're SOME crooked", then you are in a VERY bad mood!

About the Author

Necie's love of Newfoundland and Labrador comes from her wonderful memories of being raised in the outport community of St. Bernard's, Fortune Bay.

Growing up, she was part of a large and extended family, and happily spent her entire childhood in this small town.

She is passionate about this province's culture and hopes to bring the stories and traditions of the past alive, and to inspire children to love and embrace its unique heritage through her books.

Necie currently lives with her husband, children, and pets in Paradise, Newfoundland and Labrador.

Visit her personal website at:
www.overtheclothesline.com

Other Books

By Necie

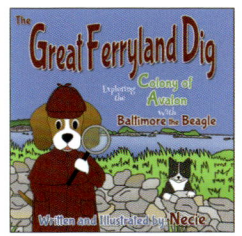

ISBN 978-1-926689-73-9

The Great Ferryland Dig

Did you ever wonder what it was like to live hundreds of years ago? Baltimore the Beagle will be you guide as you discover the Colony of Avalon, a town discovered buried under Ferryland in Newfoundland and Labrador!

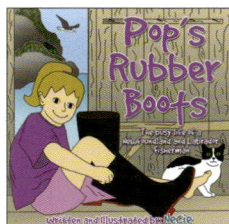

ISBN 9781926689661

Pop's Rubber Boots

Find out all about the busy life of a Newfoundland and Labrador Fisherman long ago. Discover what it means to "make fish" and to "make hay"!

ISBN 192668953-4

Bays, Bights and Tickles

Did you know there are places in Newfoundland and Labrador with names like Kettle Cove, Noddy Bay, Indian Tickle and Happy Adventure? Come along with Stewart the Seagull as he takes you to visit interesting places in Newfoundland and Labrador!

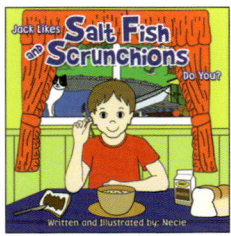

ISBN 1-92668918-6

Jack Likes Salt Fish and Scrunchions - Do You?

Come with Jack to discover some of the wonderful and unique foods of Newfoundland and Labrador and the interesting names they have! See "Scrunchion" the cat who knows everyone in town! Spot "Scrunchion" on the pages inside!

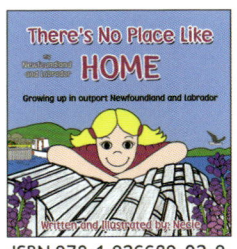

ISBN 978-1-926689-02-9

There's No Place Like My Newfoundland and Labrador Home

Find out why growing up in Newfoundland and Labrador is such a unique and wonderful experience! Spot some common Newfoundland and Labrador plants and sea creatures and discover their identity!

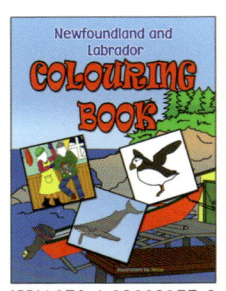

ISBN 978-1-92668957-9

Newfoundland and Labrador Colouring Book

Colour birds, sea creatures, animals and historic sites that can be found in Newfoundland and Labrador.